Assertiveness for Women

Secret Tricks to Learn How to Say No Without Feeling Guilty and Get More Respect

By
Maria Van Noord

By reading this document, the reader agrees that under no circumstances is the author responsible for any losses, direct or indirect, which are incurred as a result of the use of information contained within this document, including, but not limited to, — errors, omissions, or inaccuracies.

Table Of Contents

Chapter 1: Introduction – Types of Communication

The best place to start learning about assertiveness is to know what communication is and the different types. So, what is communication? It is the exchange or passing of thoughts, ideas, and information between two or more people.

Communication facilitates meaningful interaction among human beings. It is the process through which human beings interact with and understand each other's thoughts, ideas, opinions, and emotions. Imagine what the world would be like if we could not communicate with each other! There are primarily four types of communication, including:

1.	Passive communication
2.	Aggressive communication
3.	Passive-aggressive communication
4.	Assertive communication

Therefore, assertiveness is a personality trait that is connected to communication. Assertive communication style is characterized by a woman's ability to express her thoughts, opinions, beliefs, and emotions firmly while ensuring she does not infringe on other people's freedom to express their thoughts, opinions, beliefs, and emotions.

Edith Eva Eger, the famous Hungarian-American writer, and a Holocaust survivor, said, *"To be passive is to let others decide for you. To be aggressive is to decide for others. To be assertive is to decide for yourself. And to trust that there is enough, that you are enough."*

Assertiveness is the most preferred form because it is the most democratic style of communication. As an assertive woman, you will be able to say what you want to say and stand up for your rights without hurting people's feelings or subjugating other stakeholders' rights. A brief introduction to each of the four primary communication styles will help in improving your understanding of assertiveness.

Passive Communication

A woman with a passive communication style is one who does not stand up for her rights and beliefs. She will also not stand up for other people's rights and beliefs. A passive communicator is scared or does not have the willpower and mental strength to voice her thoughts, opinions, and emotions firmly and confidently.

As a passive communicator, even if you are hurt by other people's rude behavior or choice of words, you choose to remain silent instead of voicing your resentment. It is not that you don't want to raise your voice against injustice. You just can't find the power to do so.

A passive communicator is characterized by:
Shyness – Invariably, passive communicators are also shy, and find it difficult to speak confidently. For example, if your boss is loading you up with excessive work, then, because you are shy and don't want to attract attention to yourself, you will simply accept it instead of telling him or her that you cannot take on so much work.

Overly sensitive – Passive communicators are typically excessively sensitive to criticism and take all feedback personally. So, for example, if your husband says that the food you cooked today is not very tasty, you will be hurt, and perhaps even start crying.

Deeply self-conscious – Ask yourself if you are overly worried about how you appear in front of other people. If the answer is yes, then it is an unmistakable sign of being a passive communicator. Such people are so worried about how they will be perceived by other people that they will not do anything that might make them unpopular.

The negativities from such instances accumulate in your system in the form of anxiety, stress, and feelings of inadequacy. Soon, these accumulated negativities will breach their threshold and find unpleasant and dangerous ways of release. Eleanor Roosevelt said, *"Nobody can make you feel inferior without your consent."* Therefore, it is up to each one of you to build the necessary skills to stand up for your rights, and stop being passive communicators.

Here are some classic responses and thoughts of a passive communicator:

- I am not very smart, and therefore, I cannot be more than a housewife.

- I am not worthy of love, and that is why no one will listen to me.

- I cannot dream of going out with that good-looking colleague because I am so ugly.

- My children and my family will never think highly of me.

- I am not worthy of becoming the branch manager; I must simply be happy with my present low-level job status.

Challenges of a passive communicator:

- You will never be able to grow and develop yourself to your fullest potential.

- You will not be noticed for promotions even if you are skilled for the job.

- People will have unrealistic expectations from you, and whenever you fail to live up to these expectations, your self-belief will take a beating, resulting in low self-esteem.

- You are bound to feel that your life is not under your control.

- Your ability to mature and develop into a strong personality will be reduced considerably because your problem areas are rarely addressed.

- You are bound to suffer from depression and anxiety-related issues because of the accumulation of unnecessary negativities within your system.

Aggressive Communication

If passive communicators are at one end of the communication spectrum, passively giving in to other people's hurtful and insulting behavior, aggressive communicators are on the other end of the spectrum. They say what they want to say while violating the rights of others. Aggressive communicators are, most often, physically and/or verbally abusive.

Anne Campbell, the world-renowned British author and academic specializing in evolutionary psychology, says, *"Aggression is the first step on the slippery slope to selfishness and chaos."* People with an aggressive style of communication are characterized by:

An excessive focus on themselves – Aggressive communicators are almost always focused on themselves and have little or no regard for anyone else's views or opinions. The reason why such people choose to subjugate other people's thoughts and opinions is that they are focused on pursuing their personal agenda alone.

A woman with aggressive behavior wants only her messages and opinions to be heard, and all others' must be relegated forcefully to the background. Selfishness is one of the first attitudes that comes through in a woman behaving or communicating aggressively.

Complete lack of listening skills –Aggressive communicators' listening skills are pathetically low. Such people not only lack active listening skills but also do not have the basic listening skills needed to understand even the verbal part of the communication.

Aggressive communicators are focused only on presenting their own perspectives and viewpoints. Ironically, sometimes, they end up arguing even with those people who are actually agreeing with them! That is how poor their listening skills are.

Most often, during discussions involving an aggressive communicator, even if someone else manages to get across her viewpoint, her opinions will be rudely rejected for no rational reason.

A lack of empathy – Aggressive communicators have abysmal listening skills, and they are focused only on their personal goals. Both these attitudes are reflective of a personality that lacks empathy. Everyone else's emotions, thoughts, and pain are insignificant in the face of their selfishness.

These characteristic features of aggressive people make them appear violent, dominating, nasty, unpleasant, and insensitive.

Here are some classic responses and thoughts of an aggressive communicator:

- You are wrong, and I am right.
- I am better than you.
- I have no patience for you and your opinions.
- I must always get my way, by hook or by crook.
- I have every right to infringe upon your rights because I am superior to you.
- All the bad things happened because you did wrong, and all the right things happened because I did the right thing.

Challenges of an aggressive communicator:

•   You will alienate friends, colleagues, and after some time, even family members and loved ones, and you will find yourself alone in this wide world, having no one left in your social, personal, and professional circle to show off your aggression to.

•   Even if you have excellent oratory skills, you will not be able to win any debates because you will not be invited.

•   If you hold a position of power, you will be hated or feared; if you don't hold any position of power, you will be completely ignored. Either way, you will not find love or popularity.

•   You will never grow and develop into a mature woman because real issues in your life are bound to remain unresolved.

Passive-Aggressive Communication

As the name suggests, this style of communication combines passive and aggressive styles. Women who are passive-aggressive hide their aggressive behavior behind a façade of passivity. Have you ever felt like murdering your boss for making you do a project you hate, but outwardly, you smile at her, and say, "Okay, I will do my best?" This behavior is a classic example of passive aggression.

You can commonly see passive-aggression in your children too, especially in their interactions and behaviors with seniors, elders, and other authority figures. For example, suppose you tell your teenage daughter to clean her room before she goes out partying with her friends. You come in after a few minutes, and you are quite likely to see the room cleaner than earlier. However, you will find everything that was lying around in the room now stuffed under the bed!

She may have passively listened to your command but she used a method where her aggression got its way too. If you try arguing with her, then the typical response will be, "You are always finding fault with me no matter what I do!" People with a passive-aggressive style of communication typically exhibit the following characteristics:

They use the silent treatment very often – Sulking is one of the most common forms of passive-aggressive behavior seen in many women. Children sit grumpily, refusing to have dinner with everyone else at home, to show their displeasure.

They employ subtle insults – A colleague may appear as if she is giving you a compliment. However, if you think about it for a while, you will realize that it was a veiled insult.

They are quite vengeful – Their aggression is not entirely released from their system because they hide it well. Therefore, such people will not easily forgive and forget. They use subversive means to get revenge.

All these characteristics are noticeable by other people, and passive-aggressive communicators easily lose friends.

Here are some classic responses and thoughts of a passive-aggressive communicator:

• 	I am not angry (despite being very angry inside).

• 	Whatever! Fine!

• 	Wait, I am coming! (and taking more time than needed to come)

• 	You are always finding fault.

Challenges of passive-aggressive behavior

• Such people end up accumulating a lot of negativity within their system and becoming victims of depression and anxiety.

• Although they might release some of their negative feelings through subversive means, the root problems remain unresolved.

• Once their true nature is revealed, such people also quickly alienate others.

Assertive Communication

This form of communication is what is most sought after by people. An assertive woman says what she wants to say and provides ample space for others to voice their viewpoints, thoughts, beliefs, and opinions. Assertive women are characterized by:

Respectful behavior – Assertive people value and respect everyone's viewpoint.

Self-belief and self-worth – Assertive people identify and acknowledge their strengths and weaknesses, and therefore, have a healthy level of self-belief and self-worth.

Sincere interaction – Assertive people don't believe in fluff. They make a sincere effort to participate in all their interactions with other people.

Excellent emotional quotient – Assertive people know how to manage their emotions, and exhibit excellent self-control even during heated arguments and discussions.

Great communication skills – Assertive people understand the importance of communication skills for accurately presenting their views and thoughts. Therefore, they work hard to build their communication skills.

Here are some classic responses and thoughts of an assertive communicator:

- I am right, and so are you. Let's find a common meeting ground.
- Everyone is entitled to their opinions and thoughts.
- I speak plainly and honestly.
- I value my personal rights, and I will ensure that I don't infringe on your individual rights.

Benefits of assertiveness – Being assertive has no challenges; only benefits. Let's look at some of them:

- You will earn the respect of everyone in your personal and professional circle.
- As you address core issues of your personality and life, you will mature and develop as an individual, learning from your mistakes while accepting praise with humility.
- You will be popular and well-liked among your friends and colleagues.
- Being assertive gives you an excellent chance at leadership opportunities as most people will enjoy interacting and working for you.

Typically, men are seen as being more assertive than women. However, in modern times, this trend and perspective are changing rapidly. Many women have broken glass ceilings and have managed to become great leaders with their names deeply and inextricably etched in human history. Nearly all great women leaders have assertiveness as one of their most important and valuable traits. Building assertiveness is a critical skill in today's highly competitive environment.

Chapter 2: Why Do We Behave the Way We Do?

So, why are some of us aggressive, some of us passive-aggressive, and some of us assertive? Why do human beings behave the way we do? This chapter intends to provide some logical answers to this rather complex question.

When our ancestors were hunter-gatherers, the concept of civilization was yet unknown. Our ancestors behaved the way animals behave; exhibiting anger openly when they were angry, laughing out loud when something made them happy, crying when something made them sad, and so forth. Our ancestors lived literally from hand to mouth, eating well if they had a good hunt, and starving when they couldn't find food. They had no time or energy for anything but survival.

Gradually, human beings settled into the role of agriculturists and formed societies and civilizations. We had ample food and safe places to live, and our concerns about survival took a backseat. Now we had time for other things, and we began to look at ourselves and decided to change our behaviors to align with the changing times.

Along with many changes, we decided to change the way we expressed our emotions. We chose to categorize emotions into positive and negative. Happiness, joy, etc. were positive emotions, and anger, sadness, etc., were negative emotions. Slowly but surely, we trained ourselves to hide our negative emotions because it is considered "wrong" and "undignified" to cry during sadness or to show anger during upsetting times.

Unfortunately, human beings came to accept that suppressing emotions is the best way of handling them, and therefore, we trained ourselves and our children to hide our emotions and keep them inside. This training is one of the primary reasons for why people behave the way they do.

Our emotions are not meant to be suppressed. Our emotions work in tandem with our intelligence to help us improve our understanding of the human world and its happenings. Emotions bring music to our lives. Yes, sometimes, the music might be sad. But, many times, emotions create happiness and beauty in our lives. And we need them for our sustenance.

Moreover, emotions are nothing but a form of energy. The excess emotional energy needs to be released or dissipated into the atmosphere to prevent unpleasantness. We can use the example of a coffee percolator to understand this situation. A coffee percolator is a machine that brews aromatic, delicious coffee. How does it work? Well, you add the coffee grounds and water and switch on the percolator.

The water will boil, and the grounds will release their strength into the water, resulting in wonderful coffee. The excess energy from the boiling water needs to be released, and should not be accumulated, lest the percolator burst and splash hot, burning coffee all over, wreaking havoc on your home.

Similarly, the emotional energy from our systems needs to be released and not accumulated. When we suppress our emotions, the energy gets accumulated and is counterproductive to a happy life. When the threshold of our ability to accumulate emotional energy is reached, it will burst forth in unpleasant and dangerous ways, resulting in chaos for everyone connected with such an individual.

Gwen-Randall Young, the famous award-winning psychologist, says, *"Aggression is different from anger. Anger is an emotion; aggression is a behavior. There are better ways to deal with anger than behaving aggressively. Aggressive talk, gestures, or behaviors belong to the old way of being. Once we tune in to a higher level of consciousness, aggression is as unnecessary as is the hand-held plow in modern-day agriculture."*

Expressing our emotions maturely and productively is the best form of releasing emotional energy. Suppressing emotions is an unhealthy way of handling emotions.

Reasons for Aggressive Behavior in Women

Before we go into the reasons for aggressive behavior in women in modern times, we need to understand gender differences when it comes to aggressive behavior. Even in the contemporary world, where gender differences are considerably less than what they were a couple of decades ago, men are still allowed to exhibit aggression far more than women.

Aggression is traditionally depicted as physical or verbal abuse that tends to hurt others. Typically, men are physically stronger than women. However, in today's modern world, aggression includes non-physical qualities such as excessive ambition, competitive spirit, and assertiveness bordering on an aggressive nature; all with the intention of achieving selfish ends.

Therefore, women are also quite aggressive today and do not hesitate to reflect the aggression in their behavior and attitude. Here are some reasons for aggressive behavior in women:

Childhood environment – Most often, aggressive behavior is learned during childhood. Parents who behave aggressively pass on these habits to their children, who observe and copy parental behavior. Therefore, if a child has seen a lot of fighting and abusive behavior between her parents, invariably, she will think that it is okay to behave like that and will pick up aggressive habits.

Unresolved problems of childhood – Girls who have had an abusive childhood in any form—physical, sexual, or emotional—whose issues have remained unresolved, typically display aggressive behavior in adulthood.

Stresses of the modern world – The woman of the modern world juggles too many things for her own good, and she wants to excel in everything she does. She wants to be a supermom. She wants to break the glass ceiling at the workplace. She wants to come across as a social animal who loves to party. Excessive self-expectations and societal expectations drive many women to behave aggressively as a way of coping with stress and unrealistic expectations. The modern woman wants to be perfect in everything she does; this is an unreasonable expectation that leads to excessive stress, and unwittingly, aggressive behavior.

Additionally, PMS and menopause result in fluctuating hormones, and childbirth complexities tend to increase the aggressive streak in women today. In fact, aggressive behavior is observed to increase after childbirth because of testosterone, a hormone directly connected to aggressive behavior. Testosterone levels in men are always higher than in women, and this is one of the primary reasons used to explain the aggression inherent in men more than women.

Here is an explanation that is given by medical experts for post-pregnancy aggression. During pregnancy, testosterone levels are low in women. After childbirth, testosterone levels rise, which could be a reason for an increased aggressive behavior, post-delivery.

The desire to appear dominating – Men are traditionally considered more aggressive than women, and this reason is used many times to overlook women for promotions. Many women tend to use aggressive behavior to appear dominating so that they look capable of handling situations in the same way men do.

Low self-esteem – A woman suffering from low self-esteem uses aggression as a way to hide it from the outside world. She thinks that by showing aggressive behavior, people will think that she is strong and will not try to hurt her. Women with low self-esteem use aggressive behavior to mask their fears, insecurities, and frustrations about their own capabilities.

Reasons for Passive-Aggressive Behavior in Women

The primary difference between aggressive behavior and passive-aggressive behavior is the way the behavior is exhibited in the outside world. Women with an aggressive style of communication overtly use bad language or subjugate others' opinions and viewpoints. Passive-aggressive women behave passively but use aggressive behaviors subversively. Here are some reasons why some women choose passive-aggressive behavior over aggressive behavior:

Aggressive behavior is socially unacceptable, especially for women – While everyone, irrespective of gender, is trained to hide their negative emotions and not show aggressive behavior, women, more than men, are expected to be "ladylike" and to refrain from "unruly" behavior.

These kinds of conventional ideas are deeply entrenched in the minds of women from the time they are little girls. Therefore, many women prefer to hide their aggressive attitude behind a façade of passivity. They use subversive methods to get back at people who they believe have humiliated or insulted them. Therefore, it is common to find women colleagues carrying tales to their bosses about their coworkers while acting all nice and polite to their coworkers' faces.

Passive-aggressive behavior can be explained away easily – Muttering under one's breath, doing something wrong deliberately and then feigning an apology, etc., are easy to explain and get away with. It is very difficult to pinpoint such kinds of behaviors as wrong and pull up the people responsible for it.

For example, if you told your teenage daughter to study for her exam, she could pretend to study all night, and yet not do anything productive, right? She might be sitting at her desk with her book open, and her mind wandering somewhere else. How will you pull her up for this?

Revenge is sweet, indeed – Being vengeful is a typical trait of passive-aggressive people. They have not had the satisfaction of venting their aggressive feelings. So, they carry them around, looking for an opportune moment to get back at the person they are feeling vindictive against; because, after all, revenge is sweet.

A classic example; suppose you ask your daughter to peel the potatoes for you. There is a mound of potatoes, and she doesn't want to do the task. But she cannot openly say no, because she knows you are a strict disciplinarian. So, she will peel the potatoes in such a way that you might have to redo them! Shoddy work is a classic form of passive-aggressive behavior.

Jimmy Carter, the former US president, said, *"Aggression unopposed becomes a contagious disease."* So, heed his advice, and fight against any form of aggressive behavior you may have in your system. Instead, learn the skills of assertiveness, and get your work done nicely.

Chapter 3: Current Level of Assertiveness

Virginia Woolf said, *"Without self-awareness, we are as babies in the cradles."* Knowing yourself at a deep level is the first step to improving yourself. So, to improve your level of assertiveness, you should know where you are currently, and then make plans to move forward. This chapter, consisting of self-assessment questionnaires and quizzes, will help you gauge your current level of assertiveness. So, let's begin.

Questionnaire #1

Q1. Suppose you are waiting in line at a bank. There are people before you and after you. It is quite a long line. Now, someone walks into the bank, goes straight to the teller, and wants to be helped before the others waiting before him. Will you stand up and raise your voice against this person's actions? Y/N

Q2. You buy your husband a new cell phone for his birthday, and the salesman assures you that all the advertised features are available on the new phone. However, when your husband browses through the device, he finds a couple of features missing. Will you go back to the store (which is some distance away, and anyway, you got the phone at a huge discount) and demand an explanation or complain? Y/N

Q3. If you are angry with someone, for any reason whatsoever, do you typically express your feelings, backed by strong reasons for your anger? Y/N

Q4. You are helping your daughter with her school science project. You are a science major and know a lot about the subject. You have a big argument on the method to use for the project. Your daughter says the teacher wants it done one way, and you think it has to be done in a different way. In the end, you win the argument, and the work is completed your way. Next day, she takes the project to school and comes home with clear instructions from the teacher to redo the whole thing the same way that your daughter originally said it should be done. Will you apologize to your daughter and inform the teacher of your mistake? Y/N

Q5. If you are in a group discussion, do you make an effort to draw out people who don't appear comfortable talking or presenting their viewpoints? Y/N

Q6. Your elder sister, who has been your mentor until now, has been borrowing money from you frequently for the last couple of months. She gives some valid reasons for it. However, this time, she wants a relatively large amount, and you are concerned about her. Will you deny giving her the money and honestly explain your concerns? Y/N

Q7. If you are part of a group discussion, do you make an effort to express your viewpoints strongly? Y/N

Q8. Your new, hot neighbor has finally asked you out on a date to one of your favorite restaurants in town. You are thrilled and want to make sure nothing goes wrong. Your orders arrive, and you notice that the dish you ordered is not really what you asked for. Even at the risk of appearing unduly finicky in front of your date, will you call the waiter and ask him to get you a correctly-done order? Y/N

Q9. Do you feel comfortable asking for favors, including requests for financial help, from your friends and family? Y/N

Q10. Your son is studying for an important upcoming exam. A big group of your friends unexpectedly comes over, wanting to spend the day in your house. The noise is sure to disturb your son's study. Will you politely tell your friends to come back another day? Y/N

Q11. You have been saving money to buy that charming ruby necklace you have been eyeing at the new jewelry store. Finally, you have the money, and visit the store to pick it up. The salesgirl at the counter shows you a pair of gorgeous matching ruby earrings to go with the necklace. The addition of the pair of earrings will cost you more than you budgeted for. Will you be able to firmly say no? Y/N

Q12. Are you comfortable talking about your opinions, including sensitive matters, with your close family and friends? Y/N

Q13. Are you comfortable airing your viewpoints on sensitive matters with your colleagues? Y/N

Q14. Your old mentor is giving a presentation at your office. Suddenly, you notice she or he says something incorrectly, which could mislead everyone present. Will you stand up and correct your mentor? Y/N

Q15. You go to the local grocery store, pick up the groceries, and after paying, you take the change from the clerk without counting it, and leave the store. When you get home, you find that you were short-changed. Will you go back to the store and ask for the difference? Y/N

Q16. A relative whom you think very highly of, and who has taught you things that have helped you achieve success, comes home to visit for the first time in years. She has become old and sad. Her views have undergone huge changes (for the worse), and you are startled at the change. She says something that you disagree with strongly. In fact, it's the opposite of an idea you once learned from her. Will you express your disagreement? Y/N

Q17. An old school friend is going through a bad patch in her life. She has helped you many times in the past by lending you money. You have returned all the money owed to her. However, she still holds an important place in your heart because she helped you when you needed her the most. Now she comes to you with a request that is not just unreasonable but also illegal. Your friend says this is what she wants in return for the goodwill you have for her. Will you stand up and tell her no? Y/N

Q18. Your children, and the neighbors' kids, are trying to earn a place on the school's quiz team. There is a written quiz for the qualifying round and more than fifty students are vying for the four places. By some stroke of luck, your neighbor's children figure out the questions that are likely to be asked during the qualifying round. Your neighbor shares those questions with you so that your children and hers can both have an advantage. Will you raise your voice against this injustice and let the school know so that they can change the questions? Y/N

Q19. Your parents are going through a rough divorce, and your mother wants to come and live with you for a few months. Your house is already quite full, and you really cannot accommodate her even for a few months. Will you tell her so politely but firmly? Y/N

Q20. You and your boyfriend of many years have decided to get married, and the date is set. He is really well-to-do, and marrying him will give you a life of comfort. Thinking that he now deserves to know all about you, you tell him a couple of little-known (and embarrassing) secrets about yourself, including one that involves a dear and close friend. However, your fiancé goes around revealing this information to everyone. Will you concede that you didn't really know your boyfriend well, speak out against his betrayal, and leave him? Y/N

Q21. You and a couple of other people are patiently waiting for your turn to be helped by the lone billing clerk in a department store. A young girl walks past the line, gives the clerk an enticing look, and gets helped before all of you. Will you complain about this behavior? Y/N

Q22. One of your colleagues borrows money from you and promises to return it within a month. However, now it has been nearly two months, and there is no sign of him returning the borrowed amount. Will you approach him directly and ask for the money back? Y/N

Q23. You usually don't have a problem laughing at yourself. However, one particular day, a colleague repeatedly mocks you despite you telling him politely (and discreetly) that he is crossing the line. Will you stand up and tell him so in front of other colleagues? Y/N

Q24. You arrive late for your child's school play. She is one of the main characters in it, so you have been given a seat right in front. Will you walk right up and take your seat, knowing that everyone will see you came in late? There are vacant seats at the back that you can occupy unobtrusively. Y/N

Q25. You are discussing something personal but important with your team member. She is sharing a personal problem with you. Halfway through the discussion, your boss walks in and wants to talk about an upcoming project. Will you politely tell your boss to give you a few minutes to complete the conversation with your team member? Y/N

Questionnaire #2

Choose your most appropriate response to know what style of communication you typically use:

Q1. You are waiting in line for the bus, and someone rudely cuts in line. What will be your response?

1. Gently show the person that there is a line to be followed.

2. Give him glaring looks and "accidentally" shove him back.

3. Firmly tell the man to join his rightful place in the line.

4. Say or do nothing.

Q2. Your cousin is supposed to be coming over to your house at nine a.m. to learn a new recipe. However, she only arrives at ten. What do you do?

1. Rudely tell your cousin you don't like to be kept waiting.

2. Don't say anything, and pretend nothing has happened.

3. Ask her for a reason for her delay, and tell her not to repeat this behavior.

4. Leave the house at 9:30 so she finds it empty when she arrives.

Journaling to Gauge Your Current Level of Assertiveness

For about a month, note down details of your daily experiences. Keep track of the following points while you make entries in your journal:

- Did you state your viewpoints confidently?
- What was your communication style?

- What were your emotions?
- Do you think you managed your feelings maturely?
- Was the result of the event affected by your emotions?
- How could you have handled the situation in a better way?

When you are writing down your experiences, remember not to judge yourself. Be objective, and make copious notes of everything.

Use all three templates given in this chapter to gauge your current level of assertiveness. Make your plans to move forward from here on. Maya Angelou, one of the most brilliant women writers of modern times, said, *"When you know better, you do better."*

Chapter 4: Building Assertiveness Based On Your Core Values

Patrick Lencioni, the American writer famous for his books on business management, says, *"A core value is something that you are willing to be punished for."* Before you identify your core values, let us look at the definition of core values, and their importance in our lives.

So, what are core values? They are those qualities or personal traits that act as compasses, showing us the path to our personal goals. Core values enhance the value of your achievements and guide you through your life's path. In the absence of core values, we merely drift along, going wherever external circumstances and other people choose to take us.

The absence of core values means you are leading a directionless life. It means your life is not your own. It belongs to the person(s) who is/are leading you along. Yolanda Hadid, a popular reality TV star, says, *"I understand that my soul is my power; not my ego or perfection. If we can maintain our core values, which describe our soul, authentically, then the exteriors take second place. We find purpose in our lives."*

Importance of Core Values

Core values give our lives a sense of purpose– Core values help us make life choices that are aligned with our needs and requirements. For example, suppose family love is one of your core values, and it comes above career. Now, take an example when you have to choose between working on a weekend, because of an upcoming project, and taking your children out on a weekend picnic.

With a core value of family love being more important than career, you will easily pick taking your kids out for a weekend picnic over going to the office. That particular core value of family love gives you a sense of purpose. You purposefully choose one thing over another because you are driven by your core values.

Core values simplify our decision-making processes – Take the above example again. It is so easy to choose your kids over work because your core values are deeply entrenched in your psyche. You don't need to deliberate excessively. Look at the choices you have, see which of them are aligned with your core values, and choose accordingly. Thus, core values simplify our decision-making processes.

Core values enhance our confidence – Core values are powerful life-skill tools that give us a sense of purpose and help us lead an authentic life, driven by our souls. In such circumstances, failures and successes don't define our confidence. Living life meaningfully defines confidence, and that's what core values help us with; to live life from the depths of our souls.

Identifying Your Core Values

There are hundreds of core values from which you can choose those that best suit your lifestyle. However, instead of choosing from a predesignated list, you can discover your core values from your own experiences because core values are inherent in our personality, and all we need to do is discover, identify, and label them. Use the following template to delve deep within your soul and write your answers to the different self-assessment questions.

Recall the top-five best and happiest experiences in your life – Remember those events, and answer the following questions for each of the experiences:

Describe in detail what happened. When? What? How? Who were the other people present?

_____

_____

What were your feelings at that time?

_____

_____

What were your thoughts?

_____

_____

What were the core values that were clearly displayed during those experiences? If the event happened when you were very little, you may not have known what core values were part of the experience. However, now, reliving those experiences, you will clearly see the core values standing out.

_____

_____

Don't worry about recalling events in great detail. Just close your eyes and let your mind wander. Many of our beautiful memories are deeply etched in our minds, and when we consciously reach out to them, most of the images come forth with little or no effort. So, go ahead, give in to this self-assessment exercise, and find the answers to the questions asked.

Recall the worst or saddest five experiences of your life – Again, write down your answers to the same set of questions as above. However, the last question will be reworded as, "What are the core values that you believe were suppressed in these experiences?"

Describe in detail what happened. When? What? How? Who were the other people present?

_____

_____

What were your feelings at that time?

_____

_____

What were your thoughts?

_____

_____

What are the core values that you believe were suppressed in these experiences?

_____

_____

Next, figure out your code of conduct – Your code of conduct will be driven by those elements that make your life meaningful. After your basic survival needs are taken care of, what are the things you need to live a fulfilling life? What are the elements without which your life will feel empty and barren? You will never thrive without these items. Here are a few examples to help you understand better:

- Adventure and travel
- Learning
- Family happiness
- Career progression
- Nature
- Health and vitality
- Financial security

Write down the list of all the core values you collected – From the above three exercises, you will have acquired a fairly big list of core values. Put them all together on a piece of paper.

Combine similar values together – It is highly likely that you will have acquired a rather long list of core values. Use the list to combine similar values together. For example:

• Discipline, timeliness, dedication, commitment, etc. can be one group.

• Prayers, spirituality, wisdom, godliness, faith, etc. can also be grouped together.

Label the central theme of each group – In the above examples, discipline timeliness, dedication, and commitment can be labeled as "discipline." Prayers, spirituality, wisdom, godliness, and faith can be labeled as "faith in the divine" or "spirituality."

Create your final list of core values – From this list, take the top five to ten items. They will become your unique and personal core values. The number range five to ten is important because a list with less than five elements might not cover all life aspects, and a list with over ten elements might be so cumbersome to keep track of that it will dilute the entire exercise of creating core values for a meaningful and fulfilling life.

Rank your list of core values – Prioritize your core values based on their importance in your life. This exercise might take longer than you think because ranking a list of items, all of which appear equally important, is a big challenge. So, how do you decide which is more important than others? Here is a tip.

Recall your best and worst experiences again, and this time, focus on the intensity of the emotions you felt. The higher the intensity, the more important the emotion and the corresponding core value. The ranking is an important activity in completing an effective core value list. You will need the ranking in those situations when two or more of your core values are in conflict with each other and you feel compelled to choose one over the other.

Using Your Core Values to Enhance Your Assertiveness

Once you get your core values deeply ingrained in your psyche, you will notice that it becomes easier than before to be assertive and stand up for your beliefs and principles. The resolute clarity on your core values gives you this power. Moreover, assertiveness goes beyond being a form of communication style. Assertiveness includes other aspects of life, including:

48

Keeping our promises – Being assertive includes being self-assertive which, in turn, calls for keeping promises you make. Core values help you keep your promises because they prevent you from straying from your life's purpose.

Keeps us from having to second-guess our choices – Assertiveness includes our ability to take responsibility for our choices and not second-guess our decisions. Core values help us make clear decisions that are aligned with our life's purpose, thereby ensuring we do not need to second-guess our choices.

Keeping our commitment to our life goals – Our goals in life are nothing but our promises to ourselves. Therefore, similar to keeping promises made to other people, core values help us keep our promises to ourselves. This attitude, in turn, helps us say no to counterproductive elements that can hinder our growth and development.

Thus, discovering, identifying, and labeling your core values is, perhaps, the first and the most important step to increasing your level of assertiveness.

Chapter 5: Change Your Inner Beliefs

One of the biggest hindrances to building our assertiveness is our inner belief. As we grow and develop in human society, interacting with each other, we are taught certain things, and we think that we should live only by these beliefs.

These inner beliefs are deeply embedded in our psyche and prevent us from effecting positive changes in our lives. For example, as children, we are taught that we must not show anger because it is wrong for kids to be angry. At the time, it might make sense, because kids invariably use tantrums to show their anger. Therefore, to tell them that showing anger is unacceptable is an effective way to bring about discipline in children and to teach them the importance of managing negative emotions.

However, if this outdated lesson remains in your psyche even as a grown woman, and you simply continue to suppress negative emotions such as anger and sadness, then the coffee percolator effect is bound to negatively impact your life. Therefore, these kinds of irrelevant and valueless inner beliefs should be removed from your mindset, and replaced with relevant and sensible beliefs. Here are some inner beliefs that promote unassertive thinking and prevent us from building assertiveness:

• I should not talk about my negative emotions because it is not right to burden others with my problems.

• Asserting my opinions and thoughts might make the other person feel bad, which could ruin my good relationship with him or her.

• It is embarrassing to openly talk about feelings and emotions because they are private and meant to be hidden.

• If my friend refuses to help me once, then it means he or she doesn't like me.

• People who care about me should be able to read my thoughts, and people who don't care about me shouldn't know my thoughts. Therefore, I shouldn't be talking about my emotions.

• Saying everything I want to say is selfish.

• No one, including me, can change their mind.

• Typically, emotions should be hidden inside a person's mind.

- If I talk about fear and nervousness, then I will be seen as weak which could make people mock me.
- Accepting praise is a sign of arrogance.

In 1975, Manuel J. Smith wrote a book titled, *When I Say No, I Feel Guilty*. In that book, he proposed a "bill of assertive rights" which he believed every human being should have. The "bill of assertive rights" is a collection of inner beliefs and thoughts that promote assertiveness. Some of them include:

- Everyone, including me, has a right to be the judge of his or her own behavior, thoughts, and emotions, and to accept responsibility for their consequences.
- Everyone has a right to say no.
- There is no need to justify your actions or behavior.
- You get the power to judge other people's behavior or actions only if you take the responsibility of finding solutions to their problems.
- Everyone has the right to change his or her mind.
- Everyone has the right to choose to agree or disagree with other people's opinions.
- Everyone has the right to commit errors and to take responsibility for the consequences of those errors.
- Everyone has the right to say, "I don't know," or "I don't understand," or "I don't care."
- Everyone has the right to make illogical choices and decisions.

Changing Your Inner Beliefs

Kilroy J. Oldster, the famous trial attorney, mediator, and arbitrator, and the author of Dead Toad Scrolls, says, "Life has a tendency to provide a person with what they need in order to grow. Our beliefs, what we value in life, provide the roadmap for the type of life that we experience. A period of personal unhappiness reveals that our values are misplaced and we are on the wrong path. Unless a person changes their values and ideas, they will continue to experience discontentment."

So, to become more assertiveness than before, you must change your inner beliefs from those that promote unassertive thinking to those that promote assertive thinking. Some of us can change our inner beliefs by simply knowing and accepting that they have to be changed for our own good.

However, many of us don't have the luxury of having such a flexible mindset. We need to find reasons and evidence as to why the old inner beliefs don't make sense, and how the new inner belief will help us grow and develop our assertiveness skills. Psychologist call this approach to challenging old inner beliefs head-on, in order to change them, "disputation."

The process of disputation is based on the idea that all our inner beliefs are not facts but learned opinions. While facts cannot be changed, opinions can be easily altered to suit a particular situation. Harmful opinions need not be blindly followed. We can dispute and counter these opinions, and create new and more valuable ones than before. Thought diaries are effective means of tracking inner beliefs and raising suitable disputes to counter them.

Maintaining thought diaries – Our thoughts are not just random but nebulous, and get lost somewhere in the depths of our mind while leaving behind the emotions. Human beings have no problem handling positive emotions triggered by positive thoughts. However, we are left scrambling for cover when there is a barrage of negative emotions triggered by negative thoughts. Maintaining thought diaries is the best way to manage these random, nebulous, and highly erratic thoughts.

Let us take an illustration to help you understand how to maintain thought diaries to counter old inner beliefs. Suppose you ask a good friend to help you with some money to tide you over during a particularly bad phase in your life. She rudely says no. You are taken aback by her reaction because you believed she would help you, as you helped her earlier in the same way, So, why didn't she? Now, this is the situation we have to write our thought diary. The thought diary has two parts:

Part I requires you to write about your emotions, thoughts, and behavior.

Part II requires you to delve deep within your mind to find evidence for or against your thoughts and emotions.

Part I - Identifying your emotions – Find answers to the following questions:

What were your emotions? In addition to identifying your emotions, you must also rate them from 1 to 10; 1 being least intense and 10 being most intense. For example, if you felt anger, and the intensity rating you give is 8, then it means your anger was quite intense.

_____

_____

Part I - *Identifying your thoughts* – Find answers to the following questions:

What were your thoughts? Were you asking yourself why your friend behaved the way she did? Or were you worried that maybe she was getting back at you for something you did that hurt her? Again, rate the intensity of your thoughts from 1 to 10.

_____

_____

Part I – *Identifying your behavior* – Find answers to the following questions:

What did you do? Did you say something nasty to her? Or did you ignore her calls? Also, what were your physical sensations? Rate the intensity of your behavior from 1 to 10.

_____

_____

Follow the rule of sticking to facts while making entries in your thought diary. Do not include your opinions and interpretations. Write down only facts. For example, "My friend refused to help me with money today," is factual, whereas "My friend rudely pushed me away when I asked for money that I needed desperately," reeks of your opinion and interpretation.

Part II – Answer the following questions honestly:

What kind of communication style did I employ in this entire situation? Was it aggressive, passive, or anything else? What kind of evidence is there for this behavior?

_____

_____

Is there any evidence or proof that drove affected my emotions, thoughts, and behaviors?

_____

_____

Was I making sure that both my and my friend's assertive rights were being upheld?

_____

_____

Was I missing any element while I was undergoing the effects of my thoughts, emotions, and behaviors?

_____

_____

How could I have improved on my behavior?

_____

_____

Here are some illustrative examples for the answers that you might come up with when you reflect on the given situation:

Part I

What were your emotions? *I was angry and hurt by her refusal. Intensity of the emotion: 8*

What were your thoughts? *I was thinking, "I have helped her so many times before. She should do the same for me now." Intensity: 8*

What did you do? *When she called me after this refusal, I did not pick up her call. She called me three times, and I ignored her call all three times. I did not call her back. Intensity: 8*

Part II

What kind of communication style did I employ in this entire situation? *I was behaving in a passive-aggressive manner by not telling her about my hurt feelings in an open way, and instead, choosing to ignore her calls.*

Is there any evidence or proof that drove affected my emotions, thoughts, and behaviors? *No, there is no evidence at all. These are only my feelings and opinions*

Was I making sure that both my and my friend's assertive rights were being upheld? *No, one of the first assertive rights that I was ignoring was that everyone has a right to say no.*

Was I missing any element while I was undergoing the effects of my thoughts, emotions, and behaviors? *Yes, there have been multiple times in the past when my friend has come to my rescue. Maybe there was a really compelling reason for her to have said no to me this time.*

How could I have improved on my behavior? *I could have been more upfront, and asked her the reason for her refusal. I could have asked if she has some problems that I could help solve because her behavior was not really normal.*

After you have read your observations in Part II, try and rate the intensity of your emotions and thoughts, and you will notice that there is a considerable decrease. Therefore, using thought diaries, you can dispute your old inner beliefs and replace them relevant and useful ones. Moreover, thought diaries help you look at your emotions with an increased objectivity which, in turn, will help you manage situations more productively than before.

Chapter 6: Communication Techniques to Practice

To begin making positive changes in your communication techniques, you must first know what reasons drive people to use one or more of the four primary communication styles discussed in Chapter 1. Miranda Kerr, the famous Australian model, says, *"If you have the knowledge of how to take care of yourself, you can be a better version of yourself."*

Reasons Driving Passive Communication

- Wanting to please everyone around
- Lack of self-confidence
- Excessively worrying about whether expressed opinions will be taken the right way or not
- Excessively sensitive to criticism
- Lack of assertiveness

Reasons Driving Aggressive Communication

- Excessively focusing on achieving one's own ends with little or no empathy
- Wanting to please only oneself
- Overconfidence
- Utter disregard for others' viewpoints and opinions
- Poor listening skills

Reasons Driving Assertive Communication

- High level of confidence with no arrogance
- High level of self-awareness regarding both strengths and weaknesses
- Self-acceptance
- High level of resilience to criticism and feedback
- Always in learning mode

Here are some excellent tips and techniques that will help you improve your communication techniques for increased assertiveness.

Build Listening Skills

One of the biggest hurdles to improving assertiveness is a lack of listening skills. Most people resorting to aggressive or passive forms of communication and behavior do not have the ability to listen to what is being said in the right spirit.

Assertiveness calls for outstanding listening skills because that is what helps you discern between valuable and valueless thoughts and ideas; both your own and those of others. This discerning power allows you to make sensible assertive statements that can be accepted by all. Here are some tips to build listening skills:

Be present in the conversation – It is not just about being physically present. Your physical body, thoughts, heart, mind, and your entire being must be focused on the conversation that is taking place. Get rid of distractive elements such as your electronic devices while talking to people. Maintain healthy eye contact with the person(s) involved in the conversation so that they know that you are listening to them.

Focus on the speaker without appearing dominating or overbearing. This tip is especially important because, many times, in our earnestness to be "good listeners," we end up putting on an act of focusing excessively on the speaker which can be uncomfortable for other people.

Don't be judgmental – Everyone has a right to his or her opinion. This is one of the most important elements in the "bill of assertive rights" that was discussed in Chapter 5. Therefore, as a listener, you do not have the right to judge other people's views and opinions. Listen with an open and objective mind.

Listening without being judgmental allows you to hear viewpoints without mockery or malice. It allows you to simply respect that every opinion has something good in it. This objective perspective ensures you get the advantage of using the value in every viewpoint and idea.

Don't interrupt the speaker in the middle – When someone is talking, don't interrupt him or her to impose your solutions. It is possible that you can see a perspective relevant to the point that the speaker is talking about. He or she might have missed the point. Even in such scenarios, you must not interrupt the speaker in the middle.

Wait for the person to finish what he has to say, and then put forth your viewpoint. Abruptly interrupting a speaker sends multiple wrong messages, including:

- I don't want to listen to your ideas.
- My opinion is better (or more important) than yours.
- You are wasting my time.
- I don't care about your ideas.

All these messages, underlying your rude interruptions, are reflective of aggression. Therefore, to reduce aggression and improve assertiveness, avoid interrupting a speaker.

Identify Your Assertive Tone of Voice

In the movie *The Devil Wears Prada*, Meryl Streep speaks assertively throughout the film. She doesn't need to raise her voice to get people to obey her commands. She simply says her lines in a matter-of-fact tone that reeks of assertiveness. That is the kind of tone of voice you must identify for yourself.

Here are some tips to identify the natural tone of voice that you use in ordinary circumstances, such as asking someone at the dinner table to "pass the salt." That is the tone of voice you must identify and use in all your conversations in order to be more assertive than before. Follow these steps to identify your "pass the salt" voice:

Step #1 – Identify your natural tone of voice. For this, focus on how you say ordinary things to people. For example, if you are sitting at the dinner table, and you ask someone (anyone at the table) to pass the salt, what is your tone of voice? Focus on this tone, and learn to recognize it.

This is the most natural tone for you, and this tone is what you must use in all situations to improve your assertiveness. This natural tone of voice comes without any emotion or judgment and reflects assertiveness in the best way possible. Remember, this natural tone of voice does not hurt anyone; a key element for assertiveness.

Step #2 – Identify all the situations in your life when your tone of voice sounds "off," too loud, or too soft, driven by uncontrollable emotions. Recall these experiences and write them down. Here are some prompts to help you get started:

• What is your comfort level at a business/workplace meeting?

• How comfortable do you feel when sharing your thoughts and opinions when your bosses are present, when only your teammates are there, and when both are there?

• Do you believe your colleagues are positive when you talk at a meeting?

• How comfortable are you when talking to your loved ones and close friends (the ones you are fond of)?

- How comfortable are you when speaking to people you are not fond of?
- What is your comfort level when talking to strangers on the road whom you know you will not meet again?

Use these prompts to identify altered-voice situations. For example, if you are comfortable in an office meeting when your boss is present, what kind of voice do you use? Is it very soft, shrill, or something else? Or is it normal? In the same way, identify your tone of voice for each of the above prompts, and write it down. From these notes, you will be able to see where you are assertive and where you are not.

Step #3 – Pick out all those situations where you are not using the "pass-the-salt" voice. Typically, it means you are uncomfortable in these situations. Now, practice each of the awkward situations using your natural tone of voice. Initially, you are going to find it weird to use a natural tone of voice in situations that are emotionally charged with anger, sadness, happiness, etc.

However, don't give up. Keep practicing by saying emotion-laden and uncomfortable sentences in your normal tone of voice. With patient practice, you will realize that you can say things without raising your voice, and yet come across as assertive and firm.

Step #4 – After you have achieved a comfort level by practicing alone, use your efforts into the real-world as well. Use this normal tone of voice when you are angry with your child or spouse or someone whom you trust. They will notice the difference, and you will see whether your efforts are bearing fruit.

Alternately, practice the voice when you are talking to strangers or salespeople. For example, suppose you notice a particular salesgirl is trying to sell you something you don't want. You can feel your irritation rising. Be conscious of this emotion. Put it aside, and then deliberately use your natural tone of voice to say no to the pestering salesgirl.

In this manner, slowly practice using your "pass the salt" tone of voice in real-world situations. With some effort, you will notice that your discomfort with handling difficult situations will be considerably reduced, and your assertiveness will get a huge boost.

Learn to Say No and Use Assertive Phrases and Words

Learning to say no more often will help you make only those promises you can keep; a crucial element for assertiveness. Here are some commonly used "saying no" phrases that work in many situations. Learn them, practice them, and use them when needed:

• Thank you for offering me this opportunity; however, I am a bit tied up right now.

• Thanks for including me but I am afraid I have to pass up the offer this time.

• Thank you for reaching out to me; however, I have to say no now because I am busy with some other important work.

• This sounds like a good plan. Can I review it and get back to you in a couple of weeks?

• Thanks a lot for your opinion. Who are the other people in the group? Does anyone have a different idea?

• I disagree with you; however, you are entitled to your opinion.

• You are free to disagree with me. However, you cannot humiliate me or insult me for my views.

• I am offended by your tone of voice (or behavior or choice of words).

Learn to Handle Criticism Effectively

Assertive people handle criticism in the right spirit. They take constructive criticism seriously, but not personally, for self-improvement. They take unwarranted criticism by simply letting it go. Barbra Streisand's mother said of her daughter (long before her daughter became an icon in the film and music industry), *"She cannot be a good singer because her voice is not good, and she can't be a great actress because she is not beautiful."* We all know today how wrong this criticism was.

Barbra Streisand knew it was wrong even as a child. Instead of taking her mother's words personally, she chose to build her singing and acting skills. Like Barbra Streisand, develop your criticism-handling skills to get better at assertiveness and improve your self-learning.

Criticisms are primarily of three types, including:

1.   Criticism because of a genuine mistake
2.   Constructive criticism given by well-wishers
3.   Valueless and unfounded criticism

Let's look at how we can handle each of these:

Criticism because of a genuine mistake – We are all human beings, and being imperfect is natural to us. We all make mistakes, and if someone points out a genuine mistake, then you must accept it humbly, and thank the person for taking the trouble of pointing it out to you. Of course, after that, you must try and correct the mistake. This can be a great way of improving self-learning and getting better at your skills.

Constructive criticism given by well-wishers – Most well-wishers want only the best to happen to us. These people will leave no stone unturned (including giving you some seemingly harsh feedback) to help you achieve your potential. Criticism from well-wishers is typically constructive in nature. It is imperative that you see them for their real worth, and apply them for self-improvement and personal development. It would be foolhardy to ignore or disregard well-meant criticism from everyone, especially those who care for you.

Valueless and unfounded criticism – In the midst of all the nice people in your life, you will find those who enjoy squirming at your discomfort. Such people's criticism is typically meant to hurt or dissuade you from trying harder and getting better. It is best to ignore such forms of criticisms.

Remember Ralph Waldo Emerson's words: *"Let me never fall into the vulgar mistake of dreaming that I am persecuted whenever I am contradicted."* Take criticism in the right spirit and work on improving yourself.

Chapter 7: Tools to Build Assertiveness

Your body language and posture speak volumes about your communication style. It is possible to gauge a person's confidence and assertiveness level by the way she sits, stands, and gesticulates. For example, a passive woman will typically hunch her shoulders and sit with her head down; a symbol of uncertainty and fear. However, an assertive and confident lady will keep her shoulders straight and look into the speaker's eyes during any interaction.

Nonverbal cues, including body language, play a very important part in your communication technique. A keen observer will be able to quickly discern the more powerful team at a meeting merely by watching people's body language. Body language cues are universal and cut across geographical and cultural barriers. For example, a smile is a sign of happiness irrespective of whether you are from Africa, America, Asia, or even remote Antarctica.

Interestingly, the animal kingdom (other than humans) also uses body language to communicate. For instance, gorillas and apes expand their chest as a form of dominance over other animals. That is to say, animals present an "opening up" gesture in the form of spreading out their arms and wings to exhibit dominance and aggression.

In the same way, human beings use this "expansive" gesture to suggest dominance. Here is a classic example. Have you seen runners (especially the winners of a race) cross the finish line with their arms spread out and high above their heads, and their heads held high? That is an expansive gesture reflecting their dominance and power in that race. Watch the ones who come last in the race. You will notice their hands are hanging down at their sides, and their faces are looking down to the ground.

Similarly, have you noticed two people, belonging to different hierarchies of power, standing next to each other? Well, if you take a moment to notice it, you will realize that the two individuals complement each other's body language. For example, if you are standing next to your boss, it is very likely that your boss is standing with his hands on his (or her) hips while you are standing with your hands at your sides or clasped together in front of you; one expansive and the other subdued.

Likewise, next time, watch your boss and his boss and notice how they look when they stand next to each other. Your boss will invariably take on your posture (hands down at the sides or clasped in front), and your boss' boss will have his or her hands on his or her hips! This is a natural stance taken by human beings (and animals) who feel unequal to each other.

Power Pose for Increased Assertiveness

Multiple scientific studies have revealed that confidence and assertiveness are connected to two particular hormones: testosterone and cortisol. Testosterone is believed to be related to confidence, and cortisol is related to anxiety and stress as follows:

• The higher the level of testosterone, the higher the level of confidence

• The lower the level of cortisol, the lower the level of stress and anxiety

This relationship between testosterone and confidence, and cortisol and anxiety, is found in both men and women. Therefore, your confidence and assertiveness get a boost when testosterone levels are high and cortisol levels are low. Thus, balancing the levels of these two critical hormones in your body can have a direct impact on assertiveness.

The "power pose" is one of those postures that is believed to balance the levels of these two hormones in such a way that assertiveness and confidence are increased. The power pose is an expansive gesture (reminiscent of the expansive gestures of animals and human beings reflecting dominance and power) that takes up a lot of space and expands your body as you stretch out your arms and legs.

The psychology of the power pose is based on the concept that our behaviors drive our attitudes. Therefore, when you assume the power pose, an attitude of confidence and assertiveness is conveyed. Amy Cuddy, one of the proponents of the power pose, is a Harvard Business School professor. She says, *"Body-mind approaches such as power posing rely on the body, which has a more primitive and direct link to the mind, to tell you that you're confident."*

One of the most popular forms of power poses used to build confidence is the Wonder Woman pose. In this pose, you stand with your legs wide apart, hands on your hips, and the chin tilted slightly upward. This pose is very useful to adopt when you quickly want to build your level of assertiveness and confidence.

For example, suppose you have to give an important presentation to some senior managers in your office. You have prepared your presentation well. You have practiced really hard, and yet there is that inexplicable feeling of nervousness that is playing spoilsport.

During such times, the Wonder Woman power pose can do real wonders. Take a few minutes of solitude just before the presentation is due. Visit the restroom or find any other quiet spot. Close your eyes, focus on your breath, and physically balance yourself. Then, take the Wonder Woman power pose, and stand that way for a couple of minutes. Breathe gently, and feel the confidence rising in your body and mind. After you are satisfied with your efforts, relax, and go and make a success of your presentation.

Wrap-Up Tips to Build Assertiveness

The following points represent a short summary of the tips and tools you can use to build assertiveness (with input from this chapter and the previous one):

• You and your opinions are as valuable as everyone else's.

• Be sensible and fair in all your conversations and interactions.

- Be mindfully present in every interaction.
- Identify and practice the right (or normal) tone of voice in all uncomfortable situations.
- Don't be judgmental about anything or anyone because everyone is entitled to his or her opinion.
- Remember, your preferences, likes, and dislikes may be very different from those of other people. Being different does not mean inferior.
- Take valuable criticism seriously but not personally.
- Use the power of the Wonder Woman power pose to boost critical hormone levels that are connected to confidence and assertiveness.

Conclusion

This last chapter of the book is dedicated to listing some of the amazing benefits of assertiveness so that you can feel motivated to reread the book and redo the exercises in it to begin your journey of building assertiveness. Here are some benefits of building assertiveness:

You will not be taken for granted – Your ability to assertively state your views and opinions will ensure that no one will take you for granted; a common disadvantage with passive people.

Your popularity will soar – Your ability to listen to and accept others' viewpoints and opinions will attract more people to you, and your popularity will get a huge boost.

Your communication skills will improve considerably – Being assertive calls for developing your communication skills. As you learn and master new techniques, not only will your assertiveness get a boost, but your articulation skills will also see considerable improvement.

All your relationships will thrive – When you build your assertiveness, you also learn to respect and regard the thoughts and emotions of your partner, children, parents, colleagues, team members, and others. This positive attitude towards other people in your life will ensure that all your relationships thrive.

You will learn to manage your emotions maturely – Being assertive means you understand the havoc that unmanaged emotions can create in your life. This knowledge will drive you to learn how to manage your emotions well because of which you will handle any stressful situation with élan.

Now that you know the power of being assertive and its various benefits, it makes sense to reread the book and complete the exercises again so that you get a better understanding of how to plan your assertiveness-building path. So, go ahead, and dive head-on into the activity.

Also, you already know the deep connection that binds assertiveness to confidence and self-esteem. Therefore, if you want to receive more information and motivational tips and tricks to build confidence, self-esteem, and assertiveness, subscribe to our mailing list. Additionally, if you want to learn more about self-esteem and confidence, read the following books by the same author:

- Self-Esteem for Women
- Confidence for Women

Printed in Great Britain
by Amazon